Agony Without Relief Is Grief
A Solution for Grief, A Promise Kept

Maxwell Sears, LPC

Agony Without Relief Is Grief
A Solution for Grief, A Promise Kept
by Maxwell Sears, LPC

Copyright © 2025 Maxwell Sears, LPC

Publisher: Caya Counseling Services, Inc.

All rights reserved. No part of this publication may be reproduced, stored in a retrieval system, or transmitted in any form or by any means—for example, electronic, photocopy, recording—without the prior written permission of the publisher. The only exception is brief quotations in printed reviews.

ISBN: 978-1-7375007-1-1

Book and Cover Design: Williams DocuPrep
www.williamsdocuprep.com

Dedication

This book is dedicated to the ones whose love endures beyond absence, whose strength has lifted me through the fire, and whose presence has kept my purpose alive.

To my late mother and father, your faith, sacrifice, and truth are the roots of everything I am. Though you now dwell in eternity, your voices speak through my journey. I honor your names in every step I take and every truth I write.

To my children Wesley, Abigail, Ayana, Matthew, and Daniel Sears. Wesley, Abigail, and Ayana, your unwavering love and support have been my anchor. You stood firm while others faded. Your loyalty testifies that my legacy endures in strength and truth.

Matthew and Daniel, you are also a vital part of who I am. Each of you carries a piece of my name and purpose, and I pray this work brings you light, strength, clarity, healing, and peace for your own journey.

To all my children, know this: you are the living evidence that I have not given up or in. This work, born from agony and redeemed through faith, is my offering to you. May you find hope, courage, and truth in these pages, and may your own dash be lived with power and purpose.

This book is not just a message; it's a mantle.

Preface

This book is a labor of love. Born out of the pain of an extraordinary and talented young woman, whom I'll call Ms. Heaven to protect her identity, this book is a testament to the enduring power of hope and the transformative potential of healing. Her life, though tragically cut short, serves as a powerful catalyst for change. Her final request, 'Help them understand,' resonated deeply within me. Her plea to help others understand and heal became this book.

My own journey through grief taught me that healing requires both a map and a traveling companion. Consider this book to be both. The tools within carry Ms. Heaven's voice, forged in counseling rooms and tested in the fires of personal loss, are your lifelines. They exist because she asked.

This book is a promise kept and a guide for

those seeking to transform their pain into purpose. Healing is possible, even in the darkest of times, and hope can prevail. Let Ms. Heaven's suffering become your strength, and let these pages be your path from pain to peace. Where her earthly story ended, your healing journey can begin.

Agony Without Relief is Grief

Contents

Dedication iii

Preface v

Contents vii

Guide to Using This Book ix

Acknowledgments 1

Introduction 3

Chapter 1 ~ A Promise Kept 5

Chapter 2 ~ The Heart of Grief 12

Chapter 3 ~ The Impact of Unresolved Grief 26

Chapter 4 ~ Societal Misconceptions 37

Chapter 5 ~ Acknowledgment and Validation 47

Chapter 6 ~ Healthy Coping Mechanisms 55

Chapter 7 ~ Building a Support System 62

Chapter 8 ~ Finding Meaning and Purpose After Loss . 73

Chapter 9 ~ Professional Help and Resources 86

Chapter 10 ~ Conclusion – A Path to Healing............... 95
Life Lessons and Tools for Facing Grief 105
  Acknowledge Your Emotions: 105
  Build a Support System: 106
  Find Meaning and Purpose: 106
  Seek Professional Help: 107
  Acceptance and Action: 107
Author's Note 109
Finding Your Voice In The Reflection Of Writing........ 111
Statistics Related To Grief 117
Index 119
About The Author 121

Guide to Using This Book

1. **Receive Grace First**

   Begin with Chapter 1's story of Ms. Heaven. Let her journey soften your heart. You're not alone.

2. **Mark Grace in Margins**

   Underline every passage that speaks to your pain. God's grace meets you where you are (2 Corinthians 12:9).

3. **Practice Grace Daily**

   Use one tool per day; start with DTE in chapter 3. Grace grows through small, faithful steps.

4. **Share Grace Boldly**

   Tell one person how a lesson helped you. Grace multiplies when given away (Matthew 10:8).

5. **Become Grace's Proof**

    Journal your healing in the back pages. Your story, like Ms. Heaven's, now extends grace to others.

Acknowledgments

I extend my deepest gratitude to Ms. Heaven, whose story inspired this book and whose memory serves as a beacon of hope. Her legacy will continue to touch lives and inspire healing for generations to come.

I am also grateful to the many individuals who have shared their stories of grief and resilience, providing invaluable insights and inspiration. Your courage and vulnerability have enriched these pages and made this book possible.

Mr. Stacy Ray Bullard, thank you for the typography on the cover picture. Winefred, Willie, Pablo, and Joseph, thank you for your inspiration for the cover.

To my family and friends, thank you for your unwavering support and encouragement. Your love and understanding have sustained me through-out this journey.

To my readers, thank you for embarking on this journey of healing with me. May this book provide you with the tools and inspiration you need to navigate your own path towards wholeness and peace.

Finally, I offer my sincere thanks to all those who have contributed to the creation of this book, from editors and proofreaders to designers and publishers. Your dedication and expertise have brought this vision to life.

Introduction

Grief is not a destination but a journey. Healing is not about forgetting but about integrating loss into our lives with meaning and purpose. In the pages that follow, you will embark on a journey through the profound and often misunderstood landscape of grief. With a heart deeply touched by Ms. Heaven's final plea, Maxwell Sears offers a lifeline to those navigating the depths of sorrow.

Sears illuminates the societal misconceptions that often compound our pain, urging us to break free from the constraints of timelines and expectations. He emphasizes the importance of acknowledging our emotions, practicing self-compassion, and building a supportive community.

Through the powerful acronyms and concepts like CAYA (Come As You Are) and IAAFP

(Identification, Admittance, Acceptance, Forgiveness, Practice), BEC, and DTE, Sears provides a framework for healing that is both accessible and transformative. As you turn these pages, may you find solace, strength, and the courage to embrace your own path to healing.

Chapter 1

A Promise Kept

The darker the hour in your life the greater the victory — Caya

If you had a proven solution or plan for grief, would you use it? Well, you have that plan in your hands now.

I first met Ms. Heaven when she was assigned to edit my debut book, "Hope Without a Plan is Failure." Her insightful comments and meticulous attention to detail were invaluable. She didn't just correct grammar; she understood the essence of my writing, suggesting improvements that elevated the entire work. We'd often have long phone calls, brainstorming ideas, her voice brimming with excitement. Then, she suddenly went silent.

When I inquired why, I was told she was on leave. She had been grappling with a difficult situation. Her grandmother, her primary caregiver and a pillar of her life was gravely ill in Texas. Heaven desperately wanted to be by her side, but a crucial project deadline loomed. Her boss, a man driven by profit margins, was unsympathetic. "I wish I could go," she confided in me later, her voice trembling, "but I just can't." There's too much to do." The project, a high-profile campaign, had been under tight deadlines for months. Missing this one would mean repercussions, both for her and the team.

Heaven's life was a delicate balance of a painful tug-of-war between her work, which gave her financial security and a sense of purpose based on approval from others, and her deep love for her grandmother; she felt imprisoned and powerless.

Some choices are forced upon us, while others are made in a state of confusion, like seeing through a darkened glass. In darkness, everything looks the same. Only when light shines do we have the clarity to distinguish lies from truth and hope from hopelessness.

Through a colleague I learned that Heaven's grandmother had passed away. She had missed her chance to say goodbye. When we finally spoke, her voice was barely a whisper. "I missed her," she said. Her words heavy with regret, she said, "I missed my chance." Her grandmother, who had raised her, was her guiding light, the one who had inspired her to pursue journalism. "She was my rock," Heaven said with tears streaming down her face. "She believed in me when no one else did." Heaven became consumed by the pervasive and relentless hold of grief, and grief claimed her joy, then her hope, and finally her life.

Relationships are the cornerstone of our existence, and their loss inflicts the deepest wounds. Yet, we often prioritize unhealthy connections over healthy ones. Consider, for example, a parent trapped in an abusive relationship, believing they have no other choice, neglecting the emotional well-being of their children. This pattern of misplaced priorities is a common thread in human experience.

Heaven was overwhelmed with her grandmother's affairs. A month later, she became unreachable. I later learned that she had died, just three months after her grandmother. The news hit me like a physical blow. I couldn't comprehend that the vibrant, talented woman I knew was gone, extinguished by the weight of her grief.

Without support, grief can fester and consume us. Heaven was a maelstrom of emotions. Anger, frustration, guilt, and profound sadness consumed her. When I asked her how she was feeling, she initially gave the standard "I'm okay." But as a counselor, I recognized the facade. "I'm angry at my boss, angry at myself," she confessed, her voice thick with tears. "And I feel so guilty for not being there."

Our last conversation echoed in my mind: "Help others understand." "Help them not suffer like I did," she pleaded with a weak voice. I thought about her inability to shake the sadness and guilt. I recognized her struggle as unresolved grief. While we may never fully understand the "why" behind loss, we can learn from it. Healing begins with understanding and acknowledging the pain.

Unspoken grief carries a heavy toll. Communication, agreement, balance, change, and love are the keys to unlocking the path to healing. Acknowledging our emotions is the first step towards healing. Denial only leads to deeper despair. It's like gently waking a sleepwalker who is heading towards a precipice. Confronting our pain, however difficult, prevents us from plunging into the abyss of unresolved grief.

Heaven's story is one of unseen symbols.

- The rainbow of promise, hidden behind her storm of guilt.
- The water of release, dammed up by unspoken regrets.

- The rock of security, crumbling under societal pressures.
- The sun of growth, eclipsed by her despair.
- She missed them. You won't.

Through Heaven's pain, I remind you that you are not alone. The journey into grief begins here on these pages.

CAYA: Come As You Are

CAYA is a principle that emphasizes acceptance and non-judgment, especially when someone is seeking help. It means meeting people where they are in their grief journey, without expecting them to be "okay" or have it all together before seeking support. This is crucial because grief can be messy, and people may feel ashamed of their emotions.

Example:

A person is struggling with intense guilt after the death of a loved one and hesitates to seek counseling because they fear being judged for their "negative" feelings.

How this helps:

A counselor who embodies CAYA creates a safe space for the person to express their guilt without shame. This acceptance allows the person to confront their emotions and begin the healing process.

These tools, as presented in "Agony Without Relief is Grief," provide a comprehensive framework for understanding and navigating the complexities of grief. By applying these principles, individuals can move towards healing, growth, and a renewed sense of purpose.

Chapter 2

The Heart of Grief

*Every problem, even grief, is
fundamentally a heart problem.
— Caya*

Grief extends far beyond the loss of a loved one through death. It encompasses the loss of a job, the dissolution of a relationship, the diagnosis of a chronic illness, the struggle with addiction, and the erosion of one's sense of identity. Anticipatory grief, the sorrow felt before an impending loss, burns with a unique intensity.

Grief can manifest as an acute, searing pain or a chronic, dull ache that lingers for years. It's crucial to distinguish between grief, grievance, and grievousness. Grievance is resentment over a perceived wrong. Grievousness refers to the severity of a situation. Grief is a natural response to loss, involving various emotions and personal experiences.

Grief is a universal experience that is not limited to the death of a loved one. Grief also includes the loss of a job, the loss of a relationship, the loss of health, the loss of a limb, or the loss of finances.

Grief is the natural response to loss, and it is a learned behavior. What is learned can be unlearned, and that's why Ms. Heaven's story stands out because grief is not a mind concept; it is a HEART problem. When we do not deal with the HEART, it becomes a HARD problem, unyielding and difficult to overcome.

The mouth speaks what's in your HEART. The issues of life come out of the HEART. HEART in this context refers to the center of emotions, feelings, and intuition. It represents the core of a person's being, where love, joy, sorrow, and other emotions reside. In contrast, HARD means difficult, unyielding, or lacking in sensitivity. It implies a state that is tough to endure or overcome.

People feel with their hearts and reason with their minds. Ms. Heaven's heart was hurt, and she found no relief for that emotional pain of not being there for her grandmother as her grandmother was there for her. Her heart shut down because the agony of her pain became greater than her life.

It is not what happens to us in life, but it is how we respond with the tools we have been given. That's why in my practice as a therapist, each client is entering an apprenticeship, and the tools such as DTE, BET, ED, SPIES (see index) are tools that you will put into your tool bag so when life's challenges come, you have more than just a hammer but a multifarious set of tools. You are not living an extension of Ms. Heaven's life because she did not want others to suffer as she and her grandmother did. You now have tools that she did not have, and that can change the game of grief, grievance, and grievousness because you know what tools to use.

It is important to distinguish 'grief' from other related words.

- **Grief**: As discussed, grief is the emotional response to loss. It's a process of experiencing and coping with sorrow, sadness, and other complex emotions.

- **Grievance**: A grievance is a formal complaint or a cause of distress that provides reason for complaint or protest. For example, an employee might file a grievance against their employer due to unfair treatment.

- **Grievous**: Grievous means causing great sorrow, pain, or suffering; serious or severe. A grievous wound, for instance, is a very serious injury.

Grief is not an event; grief is a process, and every-one grieves differently because human beings live life in stages and experience different events on certain levels, and if we fail to learn from those stages, we usually have to repeat the levels, and each time we have to repeat the level, it becomes more difficult.

Consider a father whose son is battling addiction. Every day is a roller coaster of hope and despair. Even during moments of sobriety, the fear of relapse casts a long shadow, creating a persistent, gnawing grief. Or imagine someone diagnosed with a degenerative disease, grieving the loss of their physical abilities and the future they had envisioned.

Heaven understood that grief, at its core, is the absence of hope. Hope fuels faith and love. Without it, faith falters, and love becomes inaccessible. Picture a garden deprived of sunlight. The flowers wither, the leaves turn brown, and the vibrant life fades away. Similarly, without hope, our inner selves wither.

Grief often begins with a toxic cocktail of guilt, rage, and envy, blinding us to the truth. Guilt for perceived shortcomings, rage at the perceived injustice of the loss, and envy of those who haven't suffered. These emotions can culminate into a transformative pain that forces us to confront our deepest fears and vulnerabilities. Fear, in essence, stems from a lack of faith in ourselves, in others, or in a higher power.

Grief demands RELIEF. It can be relieved through:

- **Rewarding work**: Rewarding work such as volunteering at a homeless shelter or finding purpose in helping others.

- **Encouragement**: Encouragement from a friend offering a listening ear and providing words of support during a difficult time..

- **Living Intentionally**: Prioritizing time with loved ones, focusing on experiences rather than material possessions.

- **Inspiration**: Reading a book that sparks hope and resilience, listening to uplifting music.

- **Engagement**: Practicing mindfulness, staying present in the moment, engaging in creative activities.
- **Faithful Living**: Finding strength and comfort in spiritual beliefs, engaging in prayer or meditation.

While these principles are simple, implementing them requires consistent effort and dedication. Actions speak louder than words. Love without giving is empty. A parent who constantly tells their child they love them but never shows it through acts of kindness and affection fails to truly convey their love. Love and hate are mutually exclusive. We must consciously choose love. It is an act of will.

Love:
- **Listens**: Truly hearing and understanding another person's feelings, empathizing with their pain.
- **Overlooks**: Forgiving a friend's mistake, choosing to move forward rather than

holding onto resentment.

- **Values**: Recognizing the inherent worth and dignity of every individual, treating them with respect.
- **Expresses**: Showing love through acts of kindness, affection, and support.

Hate, on the other hand, is an urge to eliminate or destroy. It demands rigid boundaries and manifests as:

- **Hurt**: The emotional pain of betrayal, rejection, or abuse.
- **Anger**: The unresolved frustration that builds over time, leading to outbursts and resentment.
- **Torment**: The mental and emotional anguish of constant worry, fear, and self-doubt.
- **Emotions**: The negative feelings that consume and distort our perceptions, leading to destructive behaviors.

Behavioral words often mask some of the

deeper pain that people are sometimes too afraid to express, which supports the theme of this book that emotions are the essence of life. For example, the connection between our outward behavior and our inner emotional state.

Often, behavioral words we use to describe someone's behavior, or a surface-level observation of a person's behavior are emotions. These "behavioral words" can sometimes obscure the more profound emotional pain and destructive thinking that lies beneath the surface of behavioral words.

In society, it's common for people to use behavioral words as a substitute for expressing true emotional states. People often look for easier, more superficial terms, which can mask the complexity and intensity of what they are truly feeling.

Consider how frequently we use these words:

- **Fine**: Often used as a casual response to "How are you?" meaning "okay" or "acceptable."

- **Okay**: Similar to "fine," indicating that something is satisfactory or acceptable.

- **Great**: Used to express enthusiasm or positivity about something.

- **Good**: Indicates that something is positive or of acceptable quality.

- **Alright**: Suggests that something is acceptable or that a situation is manageable.

- **Straight**: Implies that things are in order or without problems.

- **Religious terms**: Words like "blessed," "highly favored," and "wonderful" are used to express a sense of spiritual well-being.

The key takeaway is that a person's emotions are central to their thinking and actions. To truly understand someone, we must move beyond surface-level observations and connect with their underlying feelings or emotions.

For example:

- **Aggressive**: Someone labeled as aggressive might be masking feelings of hurt, vulnerability, or fear. Their aggression could be a defense mechanism.

- **Withdrawn**: A person who is withdrawn might be experiencing deep sadness, grief, or feelings of rejection. Their withdrawal is a way to cope with overwhelming emotions.

- **Irritable**: Irritability can often be a sign of underlying anxiety, stress, or unresolved anger.

- **Numb**: When someone appears emotionally numb, it might indicate that they are experiencing a great deal of pain and have shut down as a way to protect themselves.

- **Angry**: A person experiencing anger might be reacting to a perceived injustice, a loss of control, or feelings of helplessness. This anger can manifest as irritability, aggression, or withdrawal. It's important to recognize that anger often masks other underlying emotions like hurt, sadness, or fear.

- **Sad**: Sadness is a natural response to loss, disappointment, or difficult circumstances. It can involve feelings of loneliness, emptiness, and a lack of motivation. People experiencing sadness may withdraw from social interaction, have changes in appetite or sleep, or struggle to find joy in activities they once enjoyed.

- **Fear**: Fear is often a response to perceived danger or a threat, whether real or imagined. It can trigger anxiety, worry, and a sense of vulnerability. Fear can also stem from a lack of faith or hope.

- **Hate**: Hate is a strong emotion of dislike or aversion. It can be directed towards oneself or others and can manifest as prejudice, aggression, or a desire to harm. The book also presents "HATE" as an acronym for Hurt, Anger, Torment, and Emotions.

Emotions are the essence of life. This means

that our emotional experiences are fundamental to who we are. They drive our actions, influence our thoughts, and shape our perceptions. When we focus solely on behavioral descriptions, we risk overlooking the crucial emotional component that is driving that behavior.

In the context of grief, this is particularly important. Grief is a complex and often painful emotion. People experiencing grief may exhibit a variety of behaviors such as anger, withdrawal, changes in activity levels, etc. To truly understand and help someone who is grieving, it's essential to look beyond these surface behaviors and try to connect with the underlying emotions: the sadness, the loss, the pain.

Being "ED," or emotionally dead, highlights the inability to feel another person's pain. The example of Ms. Heaven's boss illustrates this point powerfully. His focus on profit over people prevented him from empathizing with Ms. Heaven's situation, ultimately leading to a decision that disregarded her emotional needs.

It's a powerful reminder that individuals who are emotionally dead often fail to recognize or validate the emotional experiences of others. An emotionally dead person needs life, not more programs or lectures. True change comes from experiencing and engaging with life on an emotional level, and whatever a person practices, this is what he or she will become.

Detachment breeds harm. For example, a manager who avoids addressing employee conflicts, leading to resentment and decreased productivity, demonstrates this detachment.

Grief traps us in the pain of the past, preventing us from fully engaging with the present. A heart that is in grief shuts down and refuses to interact with life. Heaven surrendered to despair, allowing grief to consume her.

Challenges or difficulties can be overcome or changed, but impossibilities cannot. With faith and support, we can find the strength to overcome even the most challenging circumstances.

Chapter 3

The Impact of Unresolved Grief

Compassion is listening with your heart.— Caya

These personal stories are echoed in the broader context of our times. The grief of lost opportunities, the anxiety of an uncertain future, and the sorrow for a world forever changed are felt by many. There are tools to navigate these complex emotions for healing in a time of unprecedented grief, which we will discuss.

Financial stress often adds a significant layer of burden to grief, creating a destructive cycle. When grieving, individuals may experience:

- **Decreased Productivity**: Grief can impair focus and concentration, leading to reduced work performance and potential job loss.

- **Increased Expenses**: Funeral costs, medical bills, and other unforeseen expenses can strain financial resources.

- **Loss of Income**: The death of a primary income earner can create immediate financial hardship.

- **Difficulty Managing Finances**: Grief can make it challenging to handle financial tasks, leading to missed payments, poor investment decisions, and further stress.

- **Fear of the Future**: Uncertainty about financial stability can exacerbate anxiety and depression.

- **Dependence on others**: If a person was not financially secure before the loss, they may become dependent on other family members. This can cause additional stress.

Ms. Heaven's situation starkly illustrates the devastating impact of financial dependence. Her grandmother, her primary caregiver and guiding light, was gravely ill in Texas. Heaven desperately wanted to be by her side, but the demands of her job, the very foundation of her financial security, held her captive. Her boss, focused on deadlines and profit, would not grant her the necessary time off.

Imagine a different scenario: If Heaven had possessed financial security, she would have been liberated from this agonizing choice. She could have booked a flight to Texas without hesitation, spending precious moments with her grandmother. She would have been free from the fear of losing her job, the fear of not being able to pay her bills.

This freedom would have allowed her to:

- Provide emotional support to her grandmother during her final days.

- Say her goodbyes, alleviating the burden of regret.

- Begin the grieving process in a healthy and supportive environment.
- Avoid the crushing guilt that ultimately contributed to her own untimely death.

Heaven's story serves as a powerful reminder that financial security is not merely about accumulating wealth; it's about gaining the freedom to live a life aligned with your values. It's about having the ability to prioritize relationships and experiences over material possessions, especially during times of profound loss.

Addiction is often an attempt to numb the overwhelming emotional pain of unresolved trauma. However, it's important to broaden our understanding of addiction beyond just the loss of a loved one. As human beings, we frequently misunderstand addiction. Addiction is any behavior that we cannot let go of, especially when, as a society, we refuse to deal with the emotional connection to that addiction. It is any behavior a person cannot let go of, even when it continues to cause pain.

For example, Ms. Heaven's addiction was rooted in the pain of insecurity and the fear of failure related to her grandmother's suffering. This aligns with CAYA Counseling's perspective that the first stage of grief is guilt. In Ms. Heaven's story, we see how unresolved guilt can consume a person to the point of giving up on life. This book aims to fulfill its promise by emphasizing that words paired with inaction can be deadly.

Even the concept of SAD—Sex, Alcohol, and Drugs—can represent an addictive behavior. People often recognize that these behaviors take away the abundant life they were given, yet they struggle to stop. Anything taken to the extreme can become an addiction, with potentially deadly consequences, as illustrated in Ms. Heaven's story. Addiction also diminishes a person's sense of value. True value is the intrinsic belief that one is greater than what they are going through.

My own life serves as a living example, mirroring Ms. Heaven's story in some ways. If not for God's glory, I would not be here offering solutions to grief. In my darkest hours, when I could not feel, see, or believe, the light of Christ shone brightly. In darkness, everything appears the same; only light can distinguish joy from pain, love from hate, sadness from peace, and ultimately, life from death.

Negative thought patterns must be replaced with positive ones, and lies must be replaced with truth.

I stand here today because I found my value in Christ. One fundamental truth is that no one can alter your personal story, because it is your unique experience. Others may dislike or disbelieve it, but they cannot change it. Often, people avoid addressing the pain of life because they do not want to confront similar experiences in themselves. We become skilled at wearing behavioral masks to conceal our emotional pain.

Therapy can address the mind, provide coping strategies, and provide restructuring. However, true healing of the heart requires a deeper, spiritual transformation. Addressing symptoms without addressing the root cause ultimately fails. Negative thought patterns must be replaced with positive ones, and lies must be replaced with truth.

A counselor who focuses solely on changing a client's negative thought patterns without addressing the underlying emotional wounds will only achieve limited success.

Truth leads to healing, health, and holiness. Grief's roots—family, religion, education, community, and culture must align with spiritual, physical, intellectual, economic, and social freedom. A person who grows up in a dysfunctional family may struggle with trust and intimacy in their adult relationships. They need to shift their beliefs and behaviors to achieve emotional freedom.

Roots yield fruit. Words yield power. Choices have consequences.

Grief thrives on blame, excuses, and complaints. Choose responsibility. A person who blames their ex-partner for their failed relationship avoids taking responsibility for their own actions. They need to choose to learn from their mistakes and make different choices in the future.

True healing begins with taking responsibility for one's actions and emotions. CAYA Counseling emphasizes the importance of considering the consequences before making choices.

Roots yield fruit. Words yield power. Choices have consequences.

These are life examples that equip individuals to step out of the darkness of the world of grief and into the light of hope, which is a universal language for everyone, no matter their cultural background or religious or non-religious beliefs. Grief blinds people from the truth and hope of the power they already have inside of their heart, which are resilience, encouragement, love, inspiration, and favor to activate the tools described in this book, such as BEC: Blame, Excuse, and Complain.

BEC:

BEC represents a negative thought and behavior pattern that can hinder the grieving process. It's when someone avoids taking responsibility for their situation by blaming others, making excuses, or constantly complaining. This pattern can keep people stuck in anger and resentment, preventing them from moving forward.

Example:

A woman lost her job due to company downsizing. Instead of searching for new opportunities, she constantly blames the company, makes excuses for not updating her resume, and complains about the unfairness of the situation. *

How changing this helps:

By recognizing the BEC pattern, she can shift her focus. She can take responsibility for her job search, excuse self-pity, stop complaining and use her energy to create a great resume, and take action to find a new job. This empowers her to take control of her future and move through her grief about the job loss.

DTE: Delay, Think, and Express

DTE is a tool to help people manage their emotional responses, especially in the face of intense grief. It involves delaying the immediate reaction, taking time to think about the situation and your feelings, and then expressing yourself in a healthy way.

Example:

A man receives an insensitive comment from a relative about his grief. His initial reaction is to lash out in anger.

How this helps

Using DTE, he delays reacting, thinks about

why he's angry (hurt, feeling misunderstood), and then expresses his feelings calmly and assertively, explaining his needs to the relative. This prevents an escalation and promotes healthier communication.

Chapter 4
Societal Misconceptions

Fear is the absence of faith; hopelessness, the absence of hope. —Caya.

Society often imposes rigid and unrealistic expectations on grief, forcing individuals to suppress their emotions and adhere to an artificial timeline. This pressure to "move on" or "be strong," as seen when a grieving mother is told to suppress her pain, creates a stigma that isolates the grieving.

These societal expectations create pressure to grieve a certain way, for a certain length of time, or even dictate who is "entitled" to grieve. As a result, individuals often keep their feelings bottled up, leading to deep resentment and further compounding the stress on their physical and emotional well-being.

Key Misconceptions:
- **Grief is time-bound**: The belief that grief should resolve within a specific timeframe ignores the reality that it is a non-linear process. Research shows that grief improvement begins around six months, but it can last for years.

- **Grief follows stages**: The idea of distinct stages like denial, anger, and acceptance is misleading. Grief is a fluid mix of emotions that can occur in any order.

- **Grief is weakness**: Crying is often seen as a sign of weakness, but suppressing tears can hinder the healing process.

- **Grief is only from death**: Grief encompasses losses beyond death, including addiction, illness, career changes, and identity shifts.

- **Grief is uniform**: The misconception that everyone grieves the same way ignores the unique nature of each individual's experience.

Grief is deeply personal and immeasurable. Grief does not discriminate by age, sex, race, or socioeconomic status. Unprocessed grief leads to despair, as seen in the man who grieves the loss of his job.

The Impact of Unpracticed Healing —The CAYA Approach:

Often, we find ourselves trapped in cycles of grief because we have not practiced the skills necessary for healing, as taught by CAYA. Society's misconceptions reinforce this lack of practice, leading us to suppress emotions, deny our pain, and isolate ourselves.

Consider this: just as a musician who never practices will never master their instrument, a person who avoids practicing healthy coping mechanisms will struggle to navigate grief. We are where we are because of what we have habitually not practiced. What are the healthy coping mechanisms we habitually do not practice?

- **Emotional Expression**: Societal pressure to "be strong" prevents us from practicing healthy emotional expression. This leads to bottled-up emotions that fester and intensify over time.

- **Self-Compassion**: We are quick to judge ourselves for our grief, but we rarely practice self-compassion. This lack of self-kindness prolongs our suffering.

- **Mindfulness**: We dwell on the past or fear the future, but we rarely practice staying present. This lack of mindfulness amplifies our anxiety and distress.

- **Support-Seeking**: We believe that grief is a solitary journey, so we avoid practicing reaching out for support. This isolation deepens our sense of loneliness and despair.

Everything in life is a result of what we practice, or, in this case, what we have not practiced. We are not born with innate skills for grieving. We must cultivate them through conscious effort, aligning with the CAYA principles.

The question I put before you today is not, "What are you practicing?" but rather, "What have you neglected to practice that is keeping you trapped in your grief, hindering your journey towards CAYA (Come As You Are)?"

> *Everything in life is a result of what we practice, or have not practiced.*

By identifying these unpracticed areas, you can begin to shift your focus and cultivate the skills necessary for healing, aligning with the CAYA approach. This is not about achieving perfection, but about making consistent improvements. As long as we are alive, there is room for growth and healing, embracing the truth of

"Christ Always Your Answer."

The pressure to conform to societal expectations can cause us to hide our true feelings, leading to further isolation and pain. It is important to remember that grief is a personal journey and there is no right or wrong way to grieve. By challenging these misconceptions, we can create a more compassionate and supportive environment for ourselves and others.

Christ Always Your Answer.

This is the heart of grief: every problem has a solution, and relief starts with meeting the people where they are. Just put this tool into practice. Your mind will resist at first, but if you are persistent, your resistance will reduce because we are negative by nature, and practice the things we want to become:

RELIEF: Resilience, Encouragement, Living Intentionally, Inspiration, Engagement, Faithful Living

RELIEF is an acronym for a set of principles aimed at fostering healing and growth during grief. Each element contributes to building a stronger foundation for navigating grief.

- **Resilience**: Developing the ability to bounce back from adversity.

- **Encouragement**: Seeking and providing support.

- **Living Intentionally**: Making conscious choices aligned with values.

- **Inspiration**: Finding sources of hope and motivation.

- **Engagement**: Staying involved in life and activities.

- **Faithful Living**: Drawing strength from spiritual beliefs.

Example

A person grieving the loss of a parent feels hopeless and withdrawn.

How this helps:
Applying RELIEF, they:

- Seek encouragement from a support group (Encouragement).

- Start volunteering at an animal shelter (Rewarding Work, Engagement).

- Read inspiring books and spend time in nature (Inspiration, Living Intentionally).

- Attend church services (Faithful Living).

- They gradually build resilience and find renewed meaning.

LOVE: Listens, Overlooks, Values, Expresses

LOVE, in this context, is an acronym that describes the components of healthy love, which is presented as a powerful antidote to the destructive nature of grief.

- **Listens**: Giving full attention and empathy.

- **Overlooks**: Forgiving mistakes and moving

forward.

- **Values**: Recognizing worth and treating others with respect.

- **Expresses**: Showing love through actions and words.

Example:

A person grieving the loss of a child feels isolated because they think no one understands their pain.

How this helps: Applying LOVE, a friend:

- Truly listens without judgment to the parent's feelings (Listens).

- Forgives the parent for being withdrawn or irritable (Overlooks).

- Acknowledges the parent's strength and resilience (Values).

- Offers practical help and expresses their care (Expresses).

- This loving support helps the parent feel seen, understood, and supported in their grief.

Chapter 5

Acknowledgment and Validation

Lust is the desire to get; love, the desire to give. —Caya

Feeling grief is an act of courage, a willingness to confront the pain rather than suppress it. Journaling, mindfulness, and creative outlets can serve as powerful tools for processing emotions and facilitating healing. A man who lost his wife began journaling daily, expressing his feelings of loneliness, sadness, and anger. He found that putting his thoughts on paper helped him process his emotions and gain a deeper understanding of his grief.

Practice self-compassion, treating yourself

with the same kindness and understanding that you would offer a dear friend. Choose Christ over crisis, relying on faith to navigate the turbulent waters of grief. Grief promises comfort but delivers despair, luring us into a false sense of security.

A woman who blames herself for her divorce needs to practice self-compassion, recognizing that she did the best she could with the information and resources available to her. She can choose to rely on her faith to overcome the crisis, finding strength and guidance in her spiritual beliefs.

Grief is fundamentally a heart problem, a deep emotional wound that requires attention and care. Neglect only hardens the heart, leading to emotional detachment and isolation.

Make A Difference (MAD) by confronting your grief and choosing to heal. A person who ignores their grief after losing a parent may become emotionally distant and unable to connect with others. They need to address their grief to avoid hardening their heart.

Heaven's story serves as a tragic reminder of the gifts wasted in the graveyard of unresolved grief. Grief's empty promises rob life of its potential, leaving behind a trail of regret and what-ifs. Heaven's talents as an editor and her potential to help others were lost because she couldn't overcome her grief. Her story serves as a reminder that unresolved grief can rob us of our potential and prevent us from living a fulfilling life.

Release grief by embracing meekness, which is power under control, not weakness. Divine power transforms, allowing us to manage our emotions and respond with grace. A person who struggles with anger management learns to control their emotions through faith and self-discipline. This meekness is not weakness, but a powerful form of self-control, a conscious choice to respond with compassion and understanding.

Society often sees only behavior, not the underlying trauma that drives it. Trauma is healable, but it requires acknowledgment and validation. A person who lashes out in anger may be acting out unresolved trauma from their childhood. Society sees only the anger, not the underlying pain. With therapy, support, and a willingness to confront the past, this trauma can be healed, allowing the individual to break free from destructive patterns.

NOW: New Opportunity to Win

NOW reframes grief as a catalyst for growth. It emphasizes that grief, while painful, presents a "New Opportunity to Win" by gaining new insights and perspectives. The core idea is that setbacks are not final unless they are fatal, and action is essential for change. Even failure can lead to new beginnings.

Example:

A person loses their job and initially feels overwhelmed by grief and despair.

How this helps:

Applying NOW, they realize this loss compels them to reassess their career path. They identify their passions, acquire new skills, and start a fulfilling business. The job loss, though painful, became a "New Opportunity to Win" a more purposeful life.

Example:

A student grieves after failing an important exam, feeling like their academic dreams are shattered.

How this helps:

Embracing NOW, they view the failure as a lesson. They analyze their study habits, seek help from tutors, and develop better time-management skills. This leads to improved grades and renewed confidence.

HATE: Hurt, Anger, Torment, and Emotions

HATE is presented as a cluster of negative emotions that can hinder the healing process.

- **Hurt**: The initial emotional pain of the loss.
- **Anger**: Frustration and resentment related to the loss.
- **Torment**: The ongoing mental and emotional anguish.
- **Emotions**: The overall negative feelings that consume a person.

The book emphasizes that love cannot coexist with hate. Hate distorts a person's perception, making them believe that nothing is permanent and that they are alone, which contradicts the truth.

Example:

A person experiences betrayal in a relationship, leading to hurt, anger, and torment. They become consumed by these emotions, isolating themselves and pushing away potential new connections.

How this helps:

By recognizing the HATE pattern, they can

consciously choose love. They begin to forgive, practice empathy, and express their vulnerability in healthy ways. This allows them to heal and build trusting relationships.

Example:

Someone grieves the loss of their physical abilities due to an accident. They feel anger towards their situation and torment themselves with self-pity, hindering their rehabilitation efforts.

How this helps:

Acknowledging HATE helps them shift their focus. They choose to love themselves by practicing self-care, celebrating small victories in therapy, and expressing their feelings constructively. This empowers them to actively participate in their recovery.

These tools, NOW and HATE, provide further guidance for navigating grief. NOW offers a perspective of hope and proactive action, while understanding HATE helps individuals overcome destructive emotions and choose a path of love and healing.

Note: In each example of how people faced the process of grief and put these tools into practice to change their perspective and life, the name and story are changed to protect the innocent.

Chapter 6

Healthy Coping Mechanisms

Your problems can never overtake your blessings. —Caya

Healthy coping mechanisms are vital for navigating the turbulent waters of grief, providing anchors of stability and resilience. Physical activity, such as a daily walk in nature, releases endorphins, reduces stress, and clears the mind. Imagine Sarah, who lost her husband after a long illness. Initially, she was paralyzed by grief, unable to leave her house. But her daughter encouraged her to join a local walking group. The rhythmic motion of walking, the fresh air, and the camaraderie of others slowly began to lift her spirits. She found a sense of peace in the rhythm of her steps, a moment to breathe amidst the pain.

Nature, with its calming presence, offers solace and healing. John, grieving the loss of his childhood friend, found himself drawn to the ocean. He would sit on the beach for hours, watching the waves crash and recede, finding a parallel between the ebb and flow of the tide and his own emotions. The vastness of the ocean reminded him that his grief, though profound, was part of a larger, natural cycle.

Self-care is not selfish; it's essential for maintaining physical and emotional well-being. Maria, a single mother dealing with the loss of her job and her mother's death, initially neglected her own needs. She was constantly exhausted, her health deteriorating. Then, she decided to prioritize sleep, nutritious meals, and small pleasures like reading a book or taking a warm bath. She gradually regained her strength and resilience.

Routine provides structure and stability in the chaos of grief. After the sudden loss of his father,

David's life felt unmoored. He struggled to focus, his days blurring together. He began to implement a simple routine: waking up at the same time, exercising, working on a project, and spending time with friends. This structure helped him regain a sense of control and stability.

Support groups and new skills offer solace, purpose, and connection. Lisa, grieving the loss of her son to suicide, found comfort and understanding in a support group for bereaved parents. Sharing her experiences with others who understood her pain helped her feel less alone. She also discovered a passion for painting, taking classes and creating artwork that expressed her emotions.

Healthy coping follows the IAAFP method:
- **Identification**: Regain control by acknowledging your feelings, recognizing the specific emotions you are experiencing.
- **Admittance**: Own your actions, letting go of blame and excuses, taking responsibility for

your choices.

- **Acceptance**: Change your thinking through DTE (Delay, Think, Express), pausing before reacting, reflecting on your thoughts, and expressing your emotions in a healthy way.

- **Forgiveness**: Step into your NOW by forgiving yourself and others, releasing the burden of resentment and bitterness.

- **Practice**: Shape your character through consistent effort, making healthy coping mechanisms a regular part of your life.

Life grows from seeds. Practice hope, faith, and love, nurturing these qualities within yourself. Consistent action combats grief, preventing it from taking root and consuming your life.

Many people in daily interaction have heard that age makes maturity, and part of the Caya plan is to break hold of wrong thinking, which leads to wrongful emotions. Age does not make maturity. Maturity comes through a person accepting responsibility for his or her actions and why responsibility has both choice and consequences and dealing with the pain of grief. So, people are great at making the choice, but they do not think of the consequences. As part of the healing of grief, a person should think about consequences before the choice, and this is where:

RCC: Responsibility equals Choice and Consequence comes into play

This tool emphasizes personal accountability. It highlights that every choice we make has a consequence, and we are responsible for those consequences. In the context of grief, it means acknowledging that we choose how we respond to our grief and that those choices will influence our healing journey.

Example:

A person is grieving the death of a friend. They begin to isolate themselves, avoid social interaction, and turn to unhealthy coping mechanisms.

How this helps:

By understanding RCC, they realize that their choice to isolate has the consequence of deepening their loneliness and prolonging their grief. They can then choose to attend a support group, which has the consequence of feeling more connected and supported, aiding in their healing.

Think about consequences before the Choice

This is an extension of RCC, urging proactive consideration of the potential outcomes of our actions. It encourages foresight, especially when dealing with the emotional turmoil of grief, to make choices that support long-term well-being.

Example:

Someone is tempted to use alcohol to numb the pain of grief.

How this helps:

By thinking about the consequences before choosing, they realize that while alcohol might provide temporary relief, it can lead to addiction, health problems, and delayed emotional processing. This realization helps them choose a healthier coping mechanism, such as exercise or therapy.

Chapter 7

Building a Support System

If God takes you to it, He will take you through it. —Caya

Grief is not meant to be endured alone. Building a strong support system is crucial for navigating the challenging terrain of loss. Seek supportive individuals who offer empathy, understanding, and non-judgmental listening. Consider Emily, who, after losing her husband, felt isolated from her usual social circle. She joined a local book club, where she found new friends who listened without judgment and offered genuine support. She realized that building a support system wasn't about replacing her lost connections, but about expanding her circle of compassion.

Be honest about your needs and allow others to support you. Robert, usually a stoic and independent man, struggled to ask for help after his divorce. He felt ashamed of his vulnerability. But when a close friend offered to help him with errands and childcare, he finally accepted. He learned that asking for help was a sign of strength, not weakness, a recognition of his human need for connection and support.

Asking for help was a sign of strength, not weakness.

Join grief support groups, where you can connect with others who understand your pain and share your experiences in a safe and supportive environment. After the death of her father, a support group provided a safe space for Karen to share her feelings and experiences. She listened to others who were going through similar struggles, and their stories helped her feel less alone.

She found solace in knowing that her grief was normal and that others understood her pain.

Choose compassionate confidants, individuals who have demonstrated empathy, understanding, and a willingness to listen without judgment. After a betrayal by a close friend, Michael was hesitant to trust anyone. He carefully selected a few individuals who had demonstrated empathy and understanding in the past. He learned that quality over quantity was essential when building a support system.

Superficial connections are empty, leaving us feeling isolated and disconnected. Social media, while offering a sense of connection, can leave us feeling isolated. Sarah realized that scrolling through feeds didn't replace genuine human interaction. She began to prioritize face-to-face conversations and meaningful connections.

Grief isolates, diminishes self-worth, and creates a sense of loneliness and despair. Only God defines your worth, reminding you of your inherent value and dignity. The past teaches, the future prepares, and the NOW empowers. Your actions define your path and shape your present and future. It is crucial to remember that grief affects people of all ages. Children experience grief in unique ways, so addressing grief early in a child's life can have a profound impact on a child's outcome and foster resilience and hope to grow and build healthy relationships.

The challenges of grief in children are difficult but not impossible. These tools can be applied to help children deal with grief. The principles can equip society to help children through grief with authenticity and transparency because they equip them with the knowledge of right and wrong. So, guiding you through this is vital to development, and if you are not ready, you can lock a child in the pain of their past, not knowing how to let go of the emotional pain that plays over and over in their mind.

- Some children may have difficulty

expressing their feelings verbally.

- Some children may show grief through behavioral changes (e.g., clinginess, withdrawal, aggression, regression).
- Some children may struggle to understand the permanence of loss.
- Some may exhibit confusion and fear.
- Some may blame themselves for the loss.

Adapting the Tools for Children

We need to simplify and adapt the tools to be age-appropriate and accessible to children. Here is how:

CAYA (Come As You Are): This is especially important for children. Adults must create a safe space where children feel heard and accepted, no matter how they express their grief. This means:

- Being patient and attentive.
- Avoiding judgment or dismissal of their

feelings.

- Using simple language and validating their emotions (e.g., "It's okay to feel sad," "It's okay to miss them").

HATE: Hurt, Anger, Torment Emotions

Help children identify and express their feelings in healthy ways. Use art, play, or storytelling to help them communicate "Hurt," "Anger," "Torment" (which might manifest as confusion or fear), and other "Emotions." For example, a child can draw pictures of what they're feeling, act out their emotions with puppets, or tell a story about a character who is sad.

DTE: Delay, Think, Express

Teach children simple ways to manage their reactions.

- "Delay" can be taught as "take a deep breath" or "count to ten."

- "Think" can be simplified to "What's another way to say/do this?"

- "Express" can be guided towards healthy outlets like talking to a trusted adult, drawing, or playing.

RCC: Responsibility, Choice, Consequence

Introduce the concept of "choices and consequences" in age-appropriate terms.

For younger children, use simple cause-and-effect examples (e.g., "If you hit your brother, he will feel sad").

Relate it to grief by explaining that choosing to talk about their feelings can lead to relief, while choosing to keep them inside can lead to anxiety.

NOW: New Opportunity to Win

Focus on the idea that even though something sad happened there are still opportunities for joy and new experiences.

- Encourage children to try new activities or rediscover old hobbies.
- Celebrate small "wins" and

accomplishments to build their confidence.

RELIEF: Resilience, Encouragement, Live, Inspiration, Engagement, Faithful

Adapt the components to a child's understanding:

- **Resilience**: Help them learn to bounce back from sadness by engaging in fun activities.

- **Encouragement**: Facilitate connections with supportive people like family, friends, or teachers.

- **Living Intentionally**: Help them make choices about their day (like what to play)

- **Inspiration**: Share hopeful stories or read books about overcoming challenges.

- **Engagement**: Encourage participation in hobbies and activities.

- **Faithful Living**: For children from religious families, simple prayers or stories can provide comfort.

LOVE:

- Emphasize the importance of love and connection.
- Model loving behavior and teach children how to express love to others.
- Create a loving and supportive environment where they feel safe and secure.

Helping a Young Child Example

Six-year-old Leo's grandfather has died. He's confused, clingy, and sometimes has tantrums.

CAYA:

Leo's parents create a safe space by listening patiently to his questions, even when they are repeated. They validate his feelings, saying, "It's okay to cry. It's okay to miss Grandpa."

HATE:

They help Leo express his hurt by looking at photos of Grandpa and sharing happy memories. They address his anger (tantrums) by providing a safe outlet like hitting a pillow. They acknowledge his torment (confusion) by answering his questions honestly and simply.

DTE:

They teach Leo to "take a deep breath" when he feels upset. They encourage him to "think" about other ways to express his sadness, like drawing a picture or telling a story.

RCC:

They explain that choosing to talk about his feelings with them helps him to find relief, while choosing to keep them inside can make him anxious.

NOW:

They encourage Leo to play with his friends and try new activities. They celebrate his small achievements, reminding him that even though he's sad, he can still have fun and learn new things.

RELIEF:

The adults in a child's life can provide consistent support and love, creating a stable environment where children can feel safe to grieve and heal. Sharing stories about Grandpa can keep his memory alive.

LOVE:

The adults can shower the child with affection and teach him how to express his love for others. By adapting these tools, we can provide children with the support and guidance they need to navigate grief in a healthy way, fostering resilience and hope for the future.

Chapter 8

Finding Meaning and Purpose After Loss

Pride is absent of love as light is absent of darkness. —Caya

Meaning is personal, unique to each individual's experiences, values, and beliefs. Honor the lost through service or tributes, creating lasting legacies of love and remembrance. After her grandmother's death, Jessica created a memory garden in her backyard, planting her grandmother's favorite flowers and placing a stone with her name engraved on it. This garden became a place of reflection and remembrance, a living tribute to her grandmother's life.

Engage in fulfilling activities that bring joy,

purpose, and a sense of accomplishment. Mark, after losing his job, felt a sense of purposelessness. He decided to volunteer at a local soup kitchen, where he found fulfillment in helping others. He discovered that giving back to his community gave him a renewed sense of meaning and purpose.

Discover new talents and passions by taking up new hobbies and interests. After her divorce, Susan felt lost and adrift. She decided to take a pottery class, something she had always wanted to try. She discovered a passion for creating beautiful objects with her hands, and this new hobby gave her a sense of joy and accomplishment.

Reflect on your values, identify what truly matters to you, and align your life with those values. After a near-death experience, Thomas reevaluated his priorities. He realized that material possessions were less important than spending time with loved ones. He began to prioritize relationships and experiences over things.

Loss creates a new chapter, not a replacement. Embrace the memories and lessons learned, integrating them into your life as you move forward. After the death of her husband, Elizabeth didn't try to erase his memory. She incorporated his love and wisdom into her life. She took up his hobby of woodworking, feeling that it was a way to keep his memory alive.

Acknowledge unchangeable truths, and accept the realities of life with grace and resilience. After her diagnosis with a terminal illness, Helen accepted the reality of her situation. She focused on living each day to the fullest, appreciating the moments she had left.

Financial Security and Purpose:

One of the most significant aspects of rebuilding after loss is establishing financial security. As Ms. Heaven's story illustrates, financial dependence can lead to difficult choices and added stress during times of grief. If she had been financially secure, she might have been able to spend the time with her grandmother that she so desperately wanted. Remember, wealth without health is a nuisance, and a sound financial plan is essential for overall well-being. Financial stress is a leading cause of mental anxiety, and this book offers a path to freedom.

Here are proven strategies for building financial security:

- **Buy Stocks**: Invest in companies with growth potential, diversifying your portfolio and seeking long-term returns.

- **Buy Bonds**: Secure stable returns through government or corporate bonds, providing a reliable source of income.

- **Buy Gold**: Diversify your portfolio with a valuable asset, hedging against inflation and economic uncertainty.

- **Buy Real Estate**: Generate income and build equity through property ownership, creating a solid foundation for financial stability.

- **Build a Business**: Create your own source of income and wealth, taking control of your financial future and pursuing your entrepreneurial dreams.

These principles are not typically taught in schools, but they are crucial for achieving financial independence. CAYA uses figures like Minister Dr. Alfred Sears as an example of resilience, highlighting the importance of perseverance and determination in overcoming adversity. Regardless of the challenges you face, financial security allows you to live life on your own terms, making choices that align with your values and priorities.

The choice is yours. Don't let influence overshadow it. When we allow our emotions to get the best of us, we make poor choices. We say things we do not mean, and we do things we never thought we would do. As a result, we hurt the people we love the most, and most of all, we hurt ourselves.

Here, it's crucial to acknowledge the power of

choice and influence in navigating these emotional challenges. To admit that something is not working is one of the most humbling, fundamental, or profound choices a person can make in the short life we are given. To take action is to do something NOW: New Opportunity to Win.

Taking this a step further, a person must ask themselves "what," rather than simply "why." The "why" of life may never have a real answer, but the "what" gives you the choice to act in spite of grief or circumstances. If something is not working, the questions that should come to mind are: "Does the problem stem from me or from others in my life?" A person only has the power to change themselves. This is where choice and influence come into play.

Here are the definitions to clarify these concepts:

- **Difficulty**: Refers to something that is hard to do or accomplish; requiring effort.
- **Impossibility**: Refers to something that

cannot be done or that cannot occur.

When a person allows someone else's influence to be more powerful than their own choice, they relinquish their choice.

Here are the definitions to clarify these concepts:

- **Influence**: The capacity to have an effect on the character, development, or behavior of someone or something.

- **Choice**: An act of selecting or making a decision when faced with two or more possibilities.

The influence from others is not your choice until you succumb to it. This is a foundation of what Caya Counseling Services stands on: "Nothing in your life is final until it becomes fatal." For example, Ms. Heaven's story did not become final until the death of her grandmother, without the tools to grieve her loss.

Death is the last enemy in a person's life, so

death is not the problem, because we are all going to die. The problem is the emotional attachment a person has with death. Because death may end a life but not a relationship, however, Ms. Heaven made death greater than the life she had, so death won. The message is: whenever you make anything in life greater than God, you have no solution for what you are going through. It is the same as making influence greater than the choice you have.

Sometimes, a person will confuse difficulty with impossibility. A difficult problem can be changed; an impossibility cannot. For example, death is the greatest impossibility; no human can change it. So, if a problem is impossible, let it go. But if it is difficult, you have the power to change it or get help from someone who can. It is in silence that death consumes a life. There is power in the tongue, so open your mouth and activate the power in your heart. Go ahead, let your voice be heard, because with a voice, you have choice.

As discussed, grief is the emotional response

to loss. It's a process of experiencing and coping with sorrow, sadness, and other complex emotions. It's important to understand the various forms grief can take which include:

- **Anticipatory Grief**: Grief experienced before an impending loss, such as a terminal illness.

- **Example**: Spending quality time with a loved one with a terminal illness, expressing your feelings, and preparing for their eventual passing.

- **Complicated Grief**: Prolonged and intense grief that interferes with daily life.

- **Example**: Seeking professional therapy for prolonged sadness, inability to function, and persistent intrusive thoughts about the loss.

- **Disenfranchised Grief**: Grief that is not acknowledged or validated by society, such as the loss of a pet or a miscarriage.

- **Example**: Joining a support group for pet

loss or miscarriage, finding online communities, or journaling to validate your feelings.

- **Cumulative Grief**: Grief resulting from multiple losses over a short period.
- **Example**: Creating a timeline of losses, allowing yourself time to grieve each one individually, and seeking support to avoid emotional overwhelm.
- **Traumatic Grief**: Grief that occurs after a sudden and violent loss.
- **Example**: Seeking trauma-informed therapy, using grounding techniques to manage anxiety, and focusing on safety and stability.

Solutions for navigating grief with practical examples:

- Acknowledge and validate your feelings:
- **Example**: Instead of saying "I shouldn't feel this way," say "It's okay to feel sad, angry, or confused. My feelings are valid."

- Seek support from friends, family, or a therapist:
- **Example**: Schedule regular check-ins with a supportive friend, join a grief support group, or find a therapist specializing in grief counseling.
- Engage in healthy coping mechanisms, such as exercise, journaling, or creative expression:
- **Example**: Go for a walk or run to release pent-up energy, write down your thoughts and feelings in a journal, or express your emotions through painting, music, or other creative outlets.
- Practice self-compassion and allow yourself time to heal:
- **Example**: Treat yourself with kindness, avoid self-criticism, and allow yourself to grieve at your own pace. Don't rush the process.
- Consider therapeutic techniques like DTE,

BEC, and ED, (as mentioned earlier) to process your emotions:

DTE is Delay Think and Express if a person can delay any emotional pain in her life just for second or minute, it no longer can take control over what she does.

ED is Emotionally Dead, whenever trauma such as the death of Ms. Heaven's grandmother, she will shut down her emotions not to feel the pain of not being there before her grandmother's death, and an ED person need to embrace the pain with God's grace because she cannot do it alone.

BET is Blame, Excuses and Complain when any one blame or makes excuse or complain about what he or she is going through, she will not embrace the change that starts with accepting responsibility for she did.

These are just some of the tool that Ms. Heaven did not have for what she was going through, but we now have no excuse because you have the tool to face grief and the relief in what put into practice so her legacy to us is to stop to the cycle of grief that lead to death.

Focus on what can be changed, directing your energy towards creating the future you desire. Shape your future by making conscious choices and taking deliberate actions.

Chapter 9
Professional Help and Resources

An external solution can never solve an internal problem. —Caya

Professional help is a sign of strength, not weakness. Therapists offer tools, strategies, and a safe space to process grief and trauma. Experiencing severe anxiety after a car accident, Michael sought therapy. His therapist helped him identify and challenge his negative thought patterns, developing coping mechanisms to manage his anxiety and regain control of his life.

Cognitive Behavioral Therapy (CBT) addresses negative patterns of thinking and behavior, helping individuals to reframe their thoughts and develop healthier coping strategies. Sarah, struggling with depression after losing her job, found CBT helpful. Her therapist helped her identify the negative thoughts that were contributing to her depression and taught her how to replace them with more positive and realistic ones.

Grief counseling provides a safe and supportive environment to process grief, offering guidance and support during the healing journey. After the death of her child, a grief counselor provided a safe space for Lisa to express her emotions without judgment. The counselor helped her process her grief and develop coping strategies to navigate her loss.

Resources are available. Seek help, reach out to reputable organizations and professionals for support and guidance. After experiencing domestic violence, Jennifer found support at a local women's shelter. She learned about her rights and received counseling to help her heal from the trauma.

Healing is internal. It requires a willingness to confront your emotions and embrace vulnerability. Christ Always Your Answer, providing strength and guidance during challenging times.

Emotions must match emotions, allowing for genuine connection and empathy. Behavioral words mask pain, preventing true healing and understanding.

Heaven's story: Her past overshadowed her NOW, preventing her from fully engaging with the present. Embrace the present moment, focusing on what you can control and finding joy in the here and now.

Scenario:

Women usually see life to the lens of emotion first then thinking about what to do, and acting is the stage and if this is missed, a woman may get stuck in grieving process, and balance is the key to life and since most women are relational and giver, who usually sacrifice themselves for others. It is sometimes hard for them to receive such Helena story:

Helena is a woman in her early 40s who is grieving the end of a long-term romantic relationship. The breakup was unexpected and painful, leaving her feeling rejected, insecure, and uncertain about her future. She's struggling with intense sadness, self-doubt, and a tendency to replay negative memories.

Integrated Example:

CAYA (Come As You Are): Elena's sister, noticing her distress, approaches her with CAYA. She doesn't try to minimize Elena's pain or tell her to "just get over it." Instead, she offers a listening ear and validates Elena's feelings, saying, "It's completely understandable that you're feeling this way. Heartbreak is incredibly painful, and you don't have to pretend to be okay." This acceptance allows Elena to express her vulnerability without fear of judgment.

HATE & BEC:

Through journaling and conversations with

her sister, Elena identifies the HATE (Hurt, Anger, Torment, Emotions) and BEC (Blame, Excuse, Complain) patterns she's engaging in.

She recognizes the "Hurt" of rejection, the "Anger" at her ex-partner, the "Torment" of self-doubt, and the overwhelming "Emotions" of sadness and anxiety.

Her BEC manifests as blaming herself ("I'm not good enough"), making excuses for avoiding social situations ("I'm too tired"), and complaining about how unfair life is.

Her sister gently helps her see how these patterns are keeping her stuck in her grief.

DTE & RCC:

Elena begins to practice DTE (Delay, Think, Express) and RCC (Responsibility equals Choice and Consequence).

When she feels triggered by a memory and wants to send an angry text to her ex, she uses DTE: She **Delays** sending the text, **Thinks** about the potential consequences (more conflict, prolonged pain), and then **Expresses** her feelings in a journal entry instead.

She applies RCC to her tendency to isolate herself. She **Realizes** that her **Choice** to avoid friends has the **Consequence** of deepening her loneliness. She then chooses to attend a previously declined invitation to a dinner with friends, experiencing the positive consequence of connection and support.

NOW:

Elena starts to embrace NOW (New Opportunity to Win). She reframes the breakup as a chance for self-discovery and personal growth. She decides to take a dance class, something she's always wanted to do but never had time for in her relationship. She begins exploring new hobbies and reconnecting with old friends.

This shift in perspective helps her see that the end of the relationship, while painful, is also a

"New Opportunity" for her to create a more fulfilling life.

RELIEF:

Elena actively incorporates the principles of RELIEF:

- **Resilience**: She builds resilience by practicing self-care, setting small achievable goals, and celebrating her progress.

- **Encouragement**: She seeks support from a therapist and joins a support group for people experiencing breakups, finding validation, and understanding.

- **Living Intentionally**: She identifies her core values and makes conscious choices that align with them, such as prioritizing her well-being and personal growth.

- **Inspiration**: She reads books and listens to podcasts about overcoming adversity and building self-esteem.

- **Engagement**: She engages in activities that

bring her joy and a sense of purpose, such as volunteering at an animal shelter.

- **Faithful Living**: She draws strength from her spiritual practices, finding comfort and guidance in her faith.

LOVE:

Throughout her healing journey, Elena focuses on cultivating LOVE, both for herself and others.

- She **Listens** to her own inner voice and validates her emotions, practicing self-compassion.
- She **Overlooks** her past mistakes and imperfections, embracing self-acceptance.
- She **Values** her own strengths and unique qualities, building her self-esteem.
- She **Expresses** her love and gratitude to her friends and family, strengthening her support system.

Outcome:

By consistently using these tools, Elena navigates her grief with greater self-awareness and resilience. She moves from feeling like a victim of circumstance to feeling empowered to create a meaningful future. She learns to manage her emotions, build stronger relationships, and cultivate a deeper sense of self-love. While the pain of the breakup doesn't disappear overnight, she develops the tools to cope with it and ultimately emerges from the experience stronger and more self-assured.

Chapter 10
Conclusion – A Path to Healing

Before you can help another, you must help yourself first. —Caya

Remember, grief is a journey, not a destination, a winding path that weaves through moments of darkness and light. By acknowledging your pain, seeking support, and embracing healthy coping mechanisms, you can find a path to healing and reclaim your life. Healing is not about forgetting the person you have lost—it is about integrating their memory into your life in a meaningful way, honoring their legacy and keeping their spirit alive. You are not alone in your grief, and there is always hope for healing and a brighter future. However, the hope for healing requires action, a commitment to taking the steps necessary to move forward.

In a world where grief has become a constant companion, the need for healing is paramount. We cannot afford to ignore the emotional toll of loss, whether it is personal or collective. This book is a call to action, a reminder that healing is possible, even in the midst of profound sorrow.

Imagine telling hungry people how delicious food is, yet never feeding them—leaving them hungrier than before. But when they taste the food for themselves, they find satisfaction not in mere words, but in our actions. Likewise, our lives hold far more meaning than just grief's pain. This brief earthly journey, measured against eternity, becomes our transformative chance to live purposefully and to fully live in the NOW.

As human beings, greatness resides within us, waiting to be unleashed. Life is a gift to be embraced in each moment, and that's why some call it the "present." When it comes to truth, you have only two choices: accept it or reject it. Rejection leaves things unchanged, but acceptance is the key to transformation, allowing you to break free from the chains of grief.

The puzzle is complete, and the power is now in your hands. To move forward, these principles must not only be understood but also embraced in your heart, becoming a part of your being. The solution to grief mirrors the truth: you can either accept it or reject it. Often, we reject what we most need to embrace for change, clinging to familiar patterns of pain. Until we see the value in what we've been given, we remain stuck in the cycle of pain.

If you choose to accept the principles in this book, your life will never be the same. You will release the shame, find relief from the agony of grief, and unlock the power to truly live—not just for yourself, but to pass it forward, sharing your wisdom and compassion with others. Your life is worth it, a testament to the resilience of the human spirit.

Heaven's story serves as a powerful reminder that financial security is not merely about accumulating wealth; it's about gaining the freedom to live a life aligned with your values. It's about having the ability to prioritize relationships and experiences over material possessions, especially during times of profound loss.

If Ms. Heaven could speak to you now, she would echo this sentiment: that the pain she endured has become a promise kept, to guide and uplift those walking their own paths of grief.

The journey ahead may not be easy, but it is possible. Remember, Agony without Relief is grief—but healing is a promise fulfilled. You are not defined by your darkest hour but by your decision to rise above it. Take the tools, the truth, and the hope you now hold in your hands, and use them to shape a life full of meaning, light, and love.

The best is yet because there is resilience in you and without hope it all goes downhill from here, but thank God He has given you insight, foresight, and oversight to pick up this book to restore, to revive, and to reclaim the abundant life that was given to you over grief.

Men and women are different, but different does not mean inequality. Men have seen through different lenses than women, while men usually lead by their actions first, then their thinking, and last their emotions. Most men think emotions are female, so they do not use them, but emotions are neither male nor female but human. This leads right into Mark process through grief to:

Scenario:

Mark is experiencing grief after losing his job of 20 years. He feels a mix of anger (at the company), sadness (at the loss of his routine and identity), and fear (about his financial future).

He's been isolating himself, complaining frequently, and drinking more than usual.

Integrated Example:

CAYA (Come As You Are): Mark's friend, recognizing his struggle, approaches him with CAYA. Instead of judging Mark's negativity, the friend listens empathetically, acknowledging that it's okay for Mark to feel angry, sad, and scared. The friend validates Mark's feelings, creating a safe space for him to express his pain without feeling pressured to "be positive" immediately.

HATE and BEC:

Mark realizes, with the friend's gentle guidance, that he's stuck in HATE (Hurt, Anger, Torment, Emotions). He's also engaging in BEC (Blame, Excuse, Complain) by constantly blaming the company, making excuses for his inaction, and complaining about his situation.

The friend helps Mark identify the "Hurt" (loss of identity), "Anger" (at the company), "Torment" (worry about finances), and overwhelming "Emotions" that are driving his BEC behaviors.

Mark starts journaling to express these emotions, a healthy coping mechanism.

DTE & RCC: The friend introduces DTE (Delay, Think, Express) and RCC (Responsibility equals Choice and Consequence) to Mark.

When Mark feels the urge to lash out in anger at his family, he practices DTE: He delays his reaction, thinks about why he's angry (fear and vulnerability), and then expresses his feelings calmly, explaining his needs.

He uses RCC to recognize that his choice to isolate himself has the consequence of increasing his loneliness and depression. He realizes he's responsible for choosing healthier actions.

NOW:

Mark begins to embrace NOW (New Opportunity to Win). He reframes his job loss not just as a loss, but as a chance to explore new career paths he'd always been interested in.

He takes a course in digital marketing, something he's always wanted to learn. This gives him a sense of purpose and direction, turning his grief into a "New Opportunity."

RELIEF:

Mark actively incorporates RELIEF into his life:

- **Resilience**: He bounces back from setbacks in his job search by using DTE to manage his frustration.

- **Encouragement**: He attends a support group for job seekers, finding understanding and advice.

- **Living Intentionally**: He sets goals each day and focuses on activities that align with his values, like spending time with his children.

- **Inspiration**: He reads books about people who overcame adversity, which motivates him.

- **Engagement**: He volunteers in his community, which gives him a sense of purpose and connection.
- **Faithful Living**: He finds strength in his spiritual beliefs, which provide him with comfort and perspective.

LOVE:
- Throughout this process, Mark also focuses on LOVE.
- He **Listens** to his family's concerns without defensiveness.
- He **Overlooks** his own self-criticism and practices self-compassion.
- He **Values** his own skills and strengths, recognizing his worth beyond his job.
- He **Expresses** his love for his family and friends, strengthening his support system.

Outcome:

By consistently applying these tools, Mark

moves through his grief in a healthier way. He acknowledges his pain (CAYA), addresses his negative patterns (HATE, BEC), manages his reactions (DTE, RCC), finds new purpose (NOW), builds resilience (RELIEF), and strengthens his connections (LOVE). He still experiences sadness, but he's no longer controlled by it. He emerges from grief with new skills, a stronger sense of self, and a more fulfilling life.

Let grace carry you from agony to peace. Your journey begins now because grief is not a life sentence—it's a passage from agony to relief, and Agony Without Relief addresses grief in all forms: loss of loved ones, jobs, health, or identity because you cannot solve an internal problem with an external solution, and this book offers internal solutions for your external problems with grace: Grace wins within you NOW.

Life Lessons and Tools for Facing Grief

Acknowledge Your Emotions:

(Chapter 1, 5)

- **Lesson**: Like Heaven, suppressing emotions leads to despair. Courageously face your feelings.
- **Tool**: Journal daily, writing down your thoughts and emotions.
- **Example**: After losing her spouse, Anna initially pretended to be strong. But when she started journaling, she discovered a well of suppressed grief. Acknowledging her sadness allowed her to begin healing.

Embrace Healthy Coping Mechanisms:

(Chapter 6)

- **Lesson**: Physical activity, nature, and self-care are essential.

- **Tool**: Implement the IAAFP method: Identification, Admittance, Acceptance, Forgiveness, Practice.
- **Example**: Tom, struggling with grief, started taking long walks in the park. The fresh air and exercise helped him clear his mind and reduce his anxiety.

Build a Support System:
(Chapter 7)

- **Lesson**: You are not alone. Seek compassionate confidants.
- **Tool**: Join a grief support group or connect with trusted friends and family.
- **Example**: After losing her mother, Sarah joined a support group. Hearing others share their experiences helped her feel less isolated.

Find Meaning and Purpose:
(Chapter 8)

- **Lesson**: Honor the lost and engage in fulfilling activities.
- **Tool**: Volunteer, explore new hobbies, and

reflect on your values.

- **Example**: Michael, grieving the loss of his son, began volunteering at a local youth center. Helping others gave him a renewed sense of purpose.

Seek Professional Help:

(Chapter 9)

- **Lesson**: Therapy is a sign of strength, not weakness.
- **Tool**: Reach out to a therapist or counselor for guidance and support.
- **Example**: After experiencing severe anxiety, Lisa sought therapy. Her therapist helped her develop coping strategies and regain control of her life.

Acceptance and Action:

(Chapter 10)

- **Lesson**: Truth is a choice. Acceptance leads to transformation.
- **Tool**: Embrace the NOW (New Opportunity to Win), and take action to shape your future.

- **Example**: After years of dwelling on past regrets, David decided to focus on the present. He started practicing mindfulness and appreciating the simple joys of life.

This is your moment. The path to healing is waiting, and the power to take it is within you. Walk boldly toward the brighter future that lies ahead.

Author's Note

My value does not depend on others' opinions; my value is inherent, demonstrated by the price that was paid for me—that a person would die for me. This book extends beyond Ms. Heaven's narrative; it encompasses all of our stories—the stories of those who, despite trauma and setbacks, are still standing.

I am a living testament to a risen Savior, not because of my own actions, but because of what He has already done for me, which no one can change or diminish. When Truth enters our hearts or lives, Truth will make us either bitter or better. Through my own setbacks, I chose to become better, not bitter. Crucially, I never denied the pain, because that which is denied cannot be transformed, and it becomes hard to change.

It is not an accident that you have picked up this book. It is a divine intervention, offering you a choice between life and death. The power of choice and the answer have already been given to you: Choose life. I repeat it: Choose life over death. This is the echo of Ms. Heaven to you and from CAYA.

A final word about CAYA: To every reader—whether you are here for practical tools or spiritual hope—this acronym carries dual grace for the word CAYA, and this duality was developed out my own life experiences.

Come As You Are meets you in your grief without demands. On the other hand, Christ Always Your Answer is my personal anchor which offered **G**entleness, **R**espect, **I**nspiration, **E**ffort and **F**aith which is a relief for grief. So, take what resonates; leave what doesn't. The healing is yours to define.

Maxwell Sears, LPC

Finding Your Voice In The Reflection Of Writing

This book has explored the multifaceted nature of grief and the societal pressures that can complicate our healing, sometimes leaving us feeling voiceless. Remember, your experience is unique, and there's no 'right' way to grieve. Writing is a powerful tool for self-discovery, emotional processing, and finding your voice.

In this section, "Your Heart's Journey,' reflect on your own path." While CAYA addresses grief's heavier aspects, moments of lightness, humor, or joy are also valid. Feel free to explore these in your writing, but there's no obligation; prioritize authenticity to be free of the stigma of grief because it is too costly not to.

Prompts

1. Reflect on societal expectations about grief and if they silenced your experience.

_____
_____
_____
_____
_____
_____
_____
_____
_____
_____
_____

2. Consider moments of joy/laughter during grief. What happened? How did you feel?

_____
_____
_____
_____

Agony Without Relief is Grief

3. Write freely about your grief. Express all emotions. Include any light moments if you wish. There's no right/wrong way.

4. Reflect on a time you felt voiceless in grief. What were the circumstances? How can writing help you reclaim your voice?

5. There is no special way to write to find your voice: no voice, no choice.

_____

_____

_____

_____

_____

_____

_____

Also, consider these tools:

- **Stress Reduction**: Laughter lowers stress hormones.

- **Endorphin Release**: Laughter releases natural painkillers.

- **Immune System Boost**: Laughter enhances antibodies.

- **Pain Relief**: Laughter temporarily reduces pain.

- **Improved Mood**: Laughter alleviates anxiety/depression.

- **Social Connection**: Laughter strengthens bonds. Even in laughter there still pain to change to your gain.

Enjoy the process to find your voice. These tools will help you explore areas of grief that you had never thought possible, and it will even support you through the process of grief.

Statistics Related To Grief

- Black Americans are significantly more likely than White Americans to experience the death of a mother, father, or sibling from childhood through midlife.
- Black families have over 3 times higher odds of experiencing the death of 2 or more family members by age 30.
- By age 65, Black Americans are 90% more likely than White Americans to have experienced four or more deaths.
- Black Americans show a higher prevalence of prolonged grief disorder compared to White Americans.
- Black Americans are at higher risk for experiencing the death of a sibling or child

compared to White Americans.

- Black Americans were two and a half times more likely to lose a child by the age of 20.

- A study found a 2.5-fold increase in PGD prevalence in African and Black Americans compared to their White counterparts, with rates of 21.2% and 11.6%, respectively.

- Statistics on prolonged grief disparities among Black Americans sourced from Eterneva's research on systemic inequities in bereavement. Learn more: (https://www.eterneva.com/resources/coping-with-loss).

-

Index

Acceptance: Chapters 4, 6, 10

Addiction: Chapters 2, 3

Acknowledgment: Chapters 1, 5, 10

Anxiety: Chapters 3, 4, 9

Bereavement: Chapters 1, 3, 6, 7

CAYA (Come As You Are): Chapters 3, 4, 9, 10

CBT (Cognitive Behavioral Therapy): Chapter 9

Compassion: Chapters 3, 7

Coping Mechanisms: Chapters 3, 6, 10

Denial: Chapters 1, 4, 5

DTE (Delay, Think, Express): Chapters 6, 8

Emotions: Chapters 1, 2, 3, 5, 6, 7, 9, 10

Faith: Chapters 2, 4, 5, 6, 7, 10

Financial Security: Chapters 3, 8, 10

Forgiveness: Chapter 6

Grief: All Chapters

Guilt: Chapters 1, 2, 3, 5, 10

Healing: All Chapters

Hope: Chapters 2, 4, 6, 10

IAAFP Method: Chapter 6, 10

Journaling: Chapters 5, 10

Loss: All Chapters

Love: Chapters 2, 5, 6, 7, 10

Meaning: Chapters 8, 10

Mindfulness: Chapters 5, 6, 8, 10

NOW (New Opportunity to Win): Chapters 6, 7, 9, 10

Professional Help: Chapters 9, 10

Relationships: Chapters 1, 2, 3, 7, 8, 10

Resilience: Chapters 8, 10

Self-Compassion: Chapters 5, 6

Support System: Chapters 7, 10

Trauma: Chapters 3, 5, 9

Validation: Chapter 5

About The Author

Maxwell Sears, LPC, is a grief educator, speaker, and mental health advocate with over 20 years of experience helping people process loss and rebuild their lives. He is the author of Hope Without a Plan Is Failure, and the creator of easy-to-use tools that help readers navigate grief without needing a background in counseling or faith. Known for his warmth and honesty, Maxwell's work empowers people to move through pain with clarity, compassion, and strength.

A licensed therapist trained at Hunter College, Liberty University, and Grand Canyon University, Maxwell founded CAYA Counseling Services on one radical principle: "Come As You Are—where you will never be the same or ashamed." His DTE and BEC methods have guided thousands through the process to rediscover their strength, which lies in each of us.

Known for his warmth and honesty, Maxwell's work empowers people to move through pain with clarity, compassion, and strength.

At home with his unwavering faith echoes the promise he lives by: "The darker the hour, the greater the victory."

Contact Mr. Sears about his services or speaking engagements:

Website: cayacounselingservices.org
Email: m.sears@cayacounselingservices.org
Office: 404-324-9159

www.ingramcontent.com/pod-product-compliance
Lightning Source LLC
Chambersburg PA
CBHW071856070526
44583CB00016B/1717